BOLD IS YOUR FATE

A collection of short but vivid poems by Fortune Omosola.

(Author of Labyrinths)

Writing fulfils what money won't.

- **Fortune Omosola**

All rights reserved. No part of this publication may be reproduced, distributed, or transmitted in any form or by any means, including photocopying, recording, or other electronic or mechanical methods, without the prior written permission of the publisher, except in the case of brief quotations embodied in critical reviews and certain other non-commercial uses permitted by copyright law.

FORTUNE OMOSOLA © 2023

ISBN (Paperback) - 978-1-917267-28-1

ISBN (E-Book) - 978-1-917267-29-8

Published by Nubian Republic on behalf of Palmwine Publishing Limited Nigeria

Email: info@palmwinepublishing.com

Address- UK: 86-90, Paul Street, London EC2A 4NE

Address-Nigeria: 1A Jos Road Bukuru, Plateau State, Nigeria.

www.palmwinepublishing.com
www.raffiapress.com
www.nuciferaanalysis.com

ACKNOWLEDGEMENTS

My passion to write anything is solo. I see the world on my own and sieve through the knowledge of it, much of what I have seen, heard, known, hoping to write my hieroglyphs like distant secrets.

With love and a smile, I acknowledge my wife and two beautiful daughters, the precious gems that God gave to me.

Everything else is new and abating.

Table of Contents

Acknowledgements	3
Pale Fruits	7
In the Kings Gaze	8
Ailing Spirits	9
King David's Men	10
Pleasure Badge	12
Soaring Soul	13
My Scars	14
Feeble	15
Repine	16
Shameless Fire	17
Stealth	18
Adunni	19
Delicate Horrors	20
The Melody of a Child	21
Flowers Die	22

On Election Day	23
Man is Evil	24
Empty Troughs	25
Faithful Stranger	26
Pain	27
Generation Z	28
The Loner	29
A little King	30
Unbridled	31
Validation	32
Rendezvous	34
City People	35
The Bipolar	36
Japa	37
Nigerians	39
A Rainbow in August	40
Memory is a Lie	43
Pervert	44

The Hard Life of Mr Attention	45
The Beauty of a Thing	46
The Way of the Water	47
Time Traveller	48
Civil Soldiers	49
In the Pond	50

PALE FRUITS

Forbidden fruits, delight to worms,

old pages, bidding the storm,

the charcoal of the orient is burning,

these tales won't make it to moonlight,

but how do you win back apples without a fight?

A man is wary between the sticks,

 his lamp is the old yellow leaves in winter.

IN THE KINGS GAZE

Let your name honour the king

in the crisp of cold, warmth

before the tepid gaze of the samurai,

an unquenchable delight

Let the war chariots temper even

as you stand, intrepid.

to place your wrath

the Palace will fall

let your name honour the king

AILING SPIRITS

The spirit yawns,

enlightened? not yet,

pieces of flesh roam,

untested,

fermented in dimming corals.

KING DAVID'S MEN

With crafty hands, Benaiah held his own among David's men,

a lion died in the snow that day,

With clarity, Adino stopped the heart of eight hundred Phillistines,

He walked among dead men like it was nothing,

Before the fire walls came down on Hebron,

Samson walked past with the iron gates of Gaza,

they were lifted like chaff,

In the days of Daniel,

Shadrach led his brothers through the fire askance,

the same that consumed many by the mere thought of it,

the demeanour of Esther took sleep from King Xerxes eyes,

till she became the Queen,

a taciturn Jeremiah became an orator

the miracles of old come with lessons,

.

In Solomon was wisdom,

Abraham, blessedness,

David, a mounted wing of greatness

he, who supplied the force for army of wild beast

Adino, Eleazar, Shammah, Benaiah, Uriah, fearless destroyers whose bones were an Iron clad.

PLEASURE BADGE

I felt her in mine,

warm and supple,

a temporal journey that folds a memory

inside the brain bag

just for a moment,

it maims the panther

the one that carries the crest of fatherhood

the badge of predestination that man wears to the worms

SOARING SOUL

I have seen the flint

hurriedly so

before the sun retreats to its ancient clan

this morning, at the side of the blue flame

I felt my finger burning

smoke of my soul nurturing my blood stream

as a make a circle to part a reminder.

MY SCARS

These scars I carry are not mine,

they are cowries of encounter

my journey enlarges from here

valiant

FEEBLE

When a man loses strength,

his candle blows alone,

the wind is violent,

the water is sour,

his cup is empty,

he watches darkness morph into a porcupine

to torture his skin with a tavern sound

his skin sheds one last time.

When the dice is thrown

there are guesses

but fate has decided

and the man is all by himself

REPINE

A man comes to an end when he keeps quiet in the face of tyranny,

when he revile the truth to please himself

when he is ashamed of what puts food on his table

when he diminishes himself for pleasure.

SHAMELESS FIRE

Fire consumes the lamp,

till bubbles of sedentary soot

is darkened by it

solvent in barricades

it tries one last time

in the last chance saloon

STEALTH

When you alighted the bus that morning,

your eyes faded from its sockets,

the sole of your feet burned,

your tummy bulged as your stamped forward

frightened was your pitch as it clawed through the damp,

your innocence had fitted away by an aging cask.

ADUNNI

Adunni,

Again, you are here,

on the face of another year,

beautiful and supple,

a happy gazelle swinging through the amazon,

New heights without filters your hope can reach,

it is all in your wish.

DELICATE HORRORS

Summit horrors are for men

those who crawl get blisters

those who fly, fall,

the archives for archery are no longer symbolic

when men have learnt the secrets of aliens,

they freeze in the cold to eat the seasons frost.

THE MELODY OF A CHILD

Melodies come from children

in their laughter, in their pain

they scribble life mysteries with pencils

in their jargon, there is art

their boulevard of innocence leads

the aged from many sorrows into temporal prorogue

these melodies lose its tune on the child,

as they grow into

maleficent creatures

thronging the earth.

FLOWERS DIE

When interests are fresh, live

when they die, percieve,

Don't cook the mushrooms on stone

without a touch of liver

when the rivers side is still

find a retriever.

ON ELECTION DAY

Pick your poison,

be fast

before day breaks and you lose your fingers

before the ballot box

where thugs dressed like swine eat their breakfast

with sullen eyes and dyed teeth

their fire burns cold

harvesting tender births

for yam eaters

who you heap curses in the season of

representation

when the cycle repeats

the harvesters come with their bloody scythes,

nothing changes

except freshly marked graves.

MAN IS EVIL

An ancient curve of black,

angels melt in their snow,

planets plummet to man's

record breaking devilry

EMPTY TROUGHS

The troughs are empty,

fodder fermenting into the ground

what a waste!

a wrinkle hand hangs in the dust as chemical rain tip toes around the farm...

FAITHFUL STRANGER

I have seen your face somewhere,

I cannot remember or come further

it drowns me of my energies

my chi wriggles into an entanglement at the sight of you or your thought

your face brings memories of Sudan and the genocide in Rwanda

I will better walk on water than see your face again.

PAIN

From the flakes of fire, flames

Throwing tantrums on crusty floors

Behind the nakedness of water

Ridding itself of bleeding blisters.

GENERATION Z

The paper barely crinkles,

the pages no longer flips,

just humans in zombie form glued to digital digits

scrolling, swiping, liking

feeding a fixed smile to the algorithm

bare brains finding logic in the missing orient.

THE LONER

I am a prodigal chap

the one who almost dug the soil

but I have recovered a triple of what the master gave

on the road I have lived, ina lonely courtyard slept,

dreaming of money bags before daybreak intrudes

sometimes, I walk myself true hidden truths before it pulverises

I am somewhat an hedonist who questions everything

trying to leap while standing

I am a prodigal chap

finding answers to myths and conspiracies from the horizon of myself.

A LITTLE KING

Raise your hands and hail him

the unseen King

who kindles fire through the rough edges

and sieves water through a wine skin

bow a little and stretch a little

let him be relieved well in the warmth of your words

adore him

prostrate flat to acknowledge is unending grace.

UNBRIDLED

When I walk,

my mind levitates

ushering me to seat

imaginations are as pillars

hiding a mirror from where I gaze into gazillions

I retire to dreams in my sleep

leaping on milkyway of several inception

sometimes, wishing it to be the reality of now,

when they are scary, I choose to wake,

When I seat,

I swing in the balance of ambition

rotating under the fledging of light

carrying with me a burden of acceptance

through the lonely path of my unrighteousness.

VALIDATION

I am ashamed to talk,

Speak, walk

Tune the volume down or shout in a public place

The world is watching they say

Seeing with blind eyes and listening to nothing

I look at the sky and it's black

Unsavoury

Leaving the elements in a loop

As I wash human insatiety off my armpits

My soles touching the coals from iron base of my shoes.

The world leaves, never sorry

Leave a you hanging to the ground

And harried travelers steps you over

Unbothered

Paper cents thumbing your nose

Drowned in dye

The world misses nothing.

RENDEZVOUS

I need a dog for motivation

the one that carries me uphill

with songs from medieval piano reminiscent

in the background

these days, nothing is more cherished than a dog

loyal, bound, ominous

a leveler for a full stomach

as it barks.

CITY PEOPLE

The people of city

are never tired

yet, they pass on unnoticed

chasing the currency till it

rips power from their backs,

they survive on fumes in their iron Chambers

hard on time tail

drinking the patches

You'll need animated muscles on

to survive

to go round the cesspool

to drive the engine of wealth

the city never sleeps

but it wakes in the morning.

THE BIPOLAR

Wild is the heaven of a bipolar

in sewage for

dancing legless to the cords of internal rage

uncontrollable,

in high notes are the pitches

reaching into the abyss of the colourless

waiting for placebos.

JAPA

The sun barely shines anymore

the rain, a long wait

the land is dry and crisp,

passing faces are hard and limp

 cockroaches hold meetings in broad daylight

miles pray and mock

lets burn the currency to keep warm

before iron worms come out of it

Another chapter is here to stay, they say

On whose honour I ask?

Every man must create his own path today,

if he can't

Let's all escape to a no man's land.

If only the finger can stay a little longer on the face of the blue flame,

it will burn but find essence,

a black rot of human flesh that bluffed the frequency of pain passed by the brain

will have emerged the winner

but only if

the owner will permit the test of a cicatrix

the one that

dangles stronger than its original form.

NIGERIANS

Nigerians are lawless

they only care about their plumage

in one breath, they are the prey and the predator

ironing flesh on rotten counter

bastions of endless murmurings

they'll goad you till death

A RAINBOW IN AUGUST

The cat eyes meets the rainbow circle,

In August,

when the brown tarantula claws back to prey,

It feints in stealth, holding gaze on a cup of milk

A simple purr and its gone

A lesson has been delivered

That there is avarice in cowardice.

(This poem appears to describe a scene in nature involving a cat, a tarantula, and a rainbow. The language is metaphorical and symbolic, inviting the reader to consider deeper meanings.

The first line, "The cat eyes meets the rainbow circle," creates an image of the cat's eyes meeting the circular shape of the rainbow. This could suggest a moment of wonder or enchantment, as rainbows are often seen as magical and elusive.

The second line, "In August," sets the scene in a specific time of year, which may be significant in some way. August is typically a warm month, associated with summer and the height of nature's abundance.

The third line introduces the tarantula, which is described as having "brown claws" and as being a predator. The use of the word "prey" suggests that the tarantula is on the hunt for something to eat.

The fourth line, "It feints in stealth, holding gaze on a cup of milk," creates a sense of tension and anticipation, as the tarantula is poised to attack its prey. The cup of milk may symbolize something innocent or vulnerable, which the tarantula seeks to exploit.

The fifth line, "A simple purr and its gone," suggests that the cat has intervened and scared away the tarantula. The sound of the cat's purr is calming and unassuming, yet it has the power to frighten off the predator.

The final line, "A lesson has been delivered / That there is avarice in cowardice," offers a moral interpretation of the scene. The lesson may be that those who are greedy or selfish (avaricious) often act in a cowardly way, preying on those who are weaker or less fortunate. The cat's intervention may represent a more altruistic and courageous approach to life.

Overall, the poem offers a rich and layered meditation on nature, morality, and the power of small acts of kindness to thwart acts of violence and cruelty.)

MEMORY IS A LIE

Memory is a choice

when it travels in a time machine

a villain, when it skirts the hurricane

a hero, when it delivers packages

sometimes redolent with tears or happiness,

before it switches gear

memory is hard to contain.

PERVERT

A sumo prey in tibetan darkness

howling as a wolf

the call of orange paddings

shredded in ancient mysteries

a rumbling stomach

 raving for sparsely cuddled milk

in the serenity of winter.

THE HARD LIFE OF MR ATTENTION

Today,

attention dies

buried in a tablet

stretched in a residue

THE BEAUTY OF A THING

The beauty of a thing can vanish

if you stare too long at it,

the fine lines become soulless spirals,

blurred by the agony of self,

When you stare long enough,

a dead thing can come alive too,

rising through the ligaments of its stillness

to commune with distant variations,

revealing secrets through the crisis of conquests.

THE WAY OF THE WATER

The way of the water is elusive

illusion is born in bubbles

that shares fragrance with men

it breaks and aligns till it finds its rhyin a thousand ways down to the trench

folding spirits fly

timing the minutes of an echo

sizzled by a sword fish.

TIME TRAVELLER

Time traveler,

you are hanging on a noose.

It is hard to undo, what you wish to do,

to deconstruct a God thing with a vial,

then appear in Ephesus with a giant hour glass.

Going back won't help you,

fast forwarding is sardonic.

This appeal is not in the now when the sun fades away,

nor when you die sitting alone with the wave.

CIVIL SOLDIERS

Keep the guns blazing,

in their places, mounted,

whistling lead in forest fires,

nothing is averted,

putting paid to rotten desires,

Less is not the price.

The anchormen are busy playing aces on the pages,

till the pawns are consumed by drought,

half of what their guns fought is blood,

dripping on an open harvest of corn.

IN THE POND

The fish is hardly quiet in a still pond

its conversations are carried underneath the bubble

flirting with its tail

under the praying reed.

ABOUT THE AUTHOR

Meet Fortune Omosola, the vibrant author behind the mesmerizing book, 'The Nuances of Poetry.' With over a decade of experience in digital broadcast journalism, Fortune has left an indelible mark on the world of TV, radio and online journalism. As a seasoned news reporter, editor and on-air personality, his work is nothing short of exceptional.

However, that's not all. Fortune is a true creative at heart, with a passion for spoken word and voice over artistry. He brings a unique perspective to his writing, infusing his work with his incredible talent and captivating storytelling. In addition to this collection, Fortune is also the author of the critically acclaimed collection of poems 'Labyrinths,' published on Amazon in 2021.

With an unwavering dedication to his craft and a talent that knows no bounds, Fortune Omosola is a force to be reckoned with in the world of literature and digital journalism. His work is a true testament to the power of creativity and the impact it can have on the world around us.

F. Omosola (An honorary Professor of unconventional poetry and divisive poetic plot. He is a content creator, spoken word artist and a digital broadcast journalist)

www.ingramcontent.com/pod-product-compliance
Lightning Source LLC
Chambersburg PA
CBHW070334180426
43196CB00050B/2687